SOULSCAPES

DUAL ECHOES ONE SOUL TWO PENS

SUNITA GROVER RAINA
MANU ADIT

INDIA · SINGAPORE · MALAYSIA

Copyright © Sunita Grover Raina 2024
All Rights Reserved.

ISBN 979-8-89322-909-7

This book has been published with all efforts taken to make the material error-free after the consent of the author. However, the author and the publisher do not assume and hereby disclaim any liability to any party for any loss, damage, or disruption caused by errors or omissions, whether such errors or omissions result from negligence, accident, or any other cause.

While every effort has been made to avoid any mistake or omission, this publication is being sold on the condition and understanding that neither the author nor the publishers or printers would be liable in any manner to any person by reason of any mistake or omission in this publication or for any action taken or omitted to be taken or advice rendered or accepted on the basis of this work. For any defect in printing or binding the publishers will be liable only to replace the defective copy by another copy of this work then available.

DEDICATION

This book is dedicated to family and friends.

<u>Credits</u>:

- ❖ Marie Harris for the picture of the poetess
- ❖ Manu Adithyan for the cover designs

Soulscapes

Contents

Foreword

By Younas Rehman

Served as Director (Training) in Pakistan Railways Academy from 2010 to 2012. Retired from Railways department in 2017 as Chief Commercial Manager (Freight services and Customer Facilitation).

"Soulscapes" a poetry collection- Co-authored by Sunita Grover Raina and Manu Adit is an exquisite collection of poems that weave together the fabric of human experience with the ethereal world of souls. Sunita Grover Raina emerges as a poet of versatility, exploring the myriad facets of life, from the tangible to the philosophical, with a refreshing honesty and directness. Her poetry reflects her encounters with life, both physical and contemplative, occasionally engaging in a bold dialogue with the divine, questioning the visible and the invisible with remarkable confidence and clarity. Her unique voice stands out for its authenticity, eschewing the ornate for a more genuine expression of her inner world.

Manu Adit complements Sunita's poetic inquiries with his scholarly poise, offering profound responses that illuminate the themes explored in her verses. His contributions deepen the dialogue, bridging the personal with the philosophical, and inviting readers to ponder the essence of human experience and the nature of the soul. Together, they explore love in its myriad forms—from its joys to its sorrows—alongside meditations on philosophical and spiritual dimensions of existence.

"Soulscapes" invites readers into a conceptual realm where souls reside, probing the mysteries of existence: Is the soul a tangible entity within us, or a vast, indefinable spirit? This collection suggests a dual nature of being, where the physical and the metaphysical converge to form a complete whole. Through their poetry, Sunita and Manu navigate this intricate landscape, offering insights into the soul's place in the cosmos, touching upon the notion of time and our eternal connection to it. Study of the book in hand suggest this binary idea. One " I " of mine as I feel it as " me "and the other part being as vast, big and yet so obscure as the blend of dark matter and dark energy that make biggest part of the universe. For souls to live in bigger and yet mysterious abodes, these poems give a very fine clue.

Manu Adit's replies unfold the philosophical webs related to such questions that Sunita puts forward in her poems. What touches all of us, all times, is time itself and Sunita gives due place to time, its impacts, and its obscurities in many of her poems. Once she proclaims that she is herself time or "time-like ". Being time-like is a physical concept relating to two events taking place at different times and different locations, such that the time interval between their occurring is greater than time needed for light to reach from one event to the other. Mostly, sets of pairs of any two events occurring in our common observations are time like - and so is true for our self-conceptualization as well. Sunita seems to be thinking of living co- eternally with time. This is true in case we refer our "I" to the domain of our "soul" that nestles in grand "Soulscapes".

Manu Adit beautifully explains the queries put forth by Sunita. In one of her poems 'I Am Time', Sunita says - I, too, shall pass and never pause … I, too, am time and with a cause, I want to see the end of time …. and Manu Adit, in his reply, says: Time the silent river flows without a glance, Unmet by mortal dreams in its graceful dance ….. …… I gallop through the mists, with no path to claim, lost in the labyrinth, seeking fortune's name.

This collection is more than just a gathering of poems; it is a symphony of thoughts and emotions, a dialogue between two poets who, in their unique ways, invite us to reflect on the deeper questions of life and existence. The harmony, coherence, and empathy found within these pages are a testament to their shared journey through the vast and mysterious landscapes of the soul. Readers are sure to find resonance in this poetic assembly, a celebration of the beauty and complexity of the human spirit.

I hope readers will enjoy this collection- a poetic assembly of two beautiful poets. The harmony, coherence, and sympathy that is afforded by two poetic brooks flowing in tandem look so pretty and appealing.

Introduction

By Manu Adithyan

In the vast landscape of human connection, poetry serves as an extraordinary bridge, spanning distances both physical and emotional. It is within this ethereal realm that the paths of Sunita Grover Raina and Manu Adit serendipitously converged, crafting a narrative of resonance and harmony that culminates in the enchanting collection you now hold in your hands: Soulscapes. Imagine, if you will, two souls traversing parallel paths, separated by geography yet inexplicably drawn together by the magnetic pull of poetic expression. Sunita and Manu, strangers in the conventional sense, found themselves entwined in a dance of words upon a poetic platform. It was here that the alchemy of their connection began to unfold. Manu, inspired by the vivid imagery and poignant verses woven by Sunita, embarked on a journey of response and reflection, crafting poetic echoes that reverberated with her original compositions. Like two painters working on the same canvas, their minds intertwined, each stroke of their pens adding depth and dimension to the evolving tapestry of their collaboration. As Sunita discovered Manu's echoes resonating with her own creations, she recognized in him a kindred spirit, a fellow traveller navigating the labyrinth of human experience through the medium of verse. Despite the physical distance separating them, their shared passion for poetry transcended boundaries, weaving an invisible thread that bound their souls together. Thus, Soulscapes was born—a collection that transcends individual voices to become a harmonious symphony of shared experiences, emotions, and perspectives. Within these pages, you will find Sunita's poetic musings echoed and embellished by Manu's reverberations, each poem a testament to the profound connection forged between two kindred spirits across the expanse of space and time. In Soulscapes, the boundaries between author and responder blur, giving way to a seamless fusion of voices that speak not just to the individual, but to the collective human experience. It is a testament to the transformative power of poetry, which has the ability to bridge divides, dissolve barriers, and unite souls in a shared journey of self-discovery and expression. So, dear reader, as you embark on this poetic odyssey through the landscapes of the soul, may you find solace, inspiration, and companionship in the words of Sunita Grover Raina and Manu Adit. For in their collaboration lies a timeless reminder that true connection knows no bounds—it is a melody that resonates across the vast expanse of the human heart.

$\mathcal{S}$OULSCAPES

(POEM -1) Sunita Grover Raina & Manu Adithyan

PLEASE ANSWER

I took out my cycle
for a ride to the past
I found myself standing
So were the surroundings

But they all had moved
I came here to collect the answers
If they had left behind

Maybe if things had changed
Maybe in my ways rearranged

Maybe if things had been agreed to
My explanations accepted and my innocence
proved

But where are they
They seemed to have moved away
Should I ride my cycle to the future then?
Wish they had left a note as to when

It is so tiring to search them out
Why none of them for me fought
Why was I not understood
I spoke honestly, to them was good

Things were not so complicated
Or were they not interested
Was it their plan to get me alienated
And I a fool still wanting to be oriented.

©Sunita Grover Raina
India.

ECHOED BY HIM

Upon the road of memories, I took my faithful steed
Seeking solace in the past, hoping my wounds to heed

But time had played its tricks, and left me in dismay
For everyone had vanished, leaving me astray

I yearned for understanding, for answers to my plight
Hoping they'd be waiting, in the fading twilight.

But silence was my answer, as emptiness prevailed
Leaving me to wonder if my efforts had just failed

Should I turn my handlebars, and ride into the unknown?
Seeking solace in the future, where seeds of hope are sown

If only they had left a sign, a clue to ease my mind
But their absence speaks loudly, leaving me behind

It's exhausting to pursue them, through the
labyrinth of doubt
Wondering why they left, what love they were
without

I spoke my truth sincerely, yet they turned a
deafened ear
Leaving me to ponder if their hearts were
insincere

Were things truly so complex, or did they
simply not care?
Was my exile their design, a burden I must bear?

Am I the fool for longing, to bridge this great
divide
Hoping for reconciliation, with hearts so cold
and wide?

So I peddle through the echoes, of a past that's
left me stained
Hoping for redemption, in a world that's often
pained

Though the road is long and lonely, and the
shadows ever tall
I'll ride on in search of peace, until I find my
soul's recall.

@Manu Adit
Dubai (UAE)

(POEM -2) Sunita Grover Raina & Manu Adithyan

OH! WHAT A SHAME

Love is not to blame
Why give it names
When it is the mind
that plays games
We bloom it, we nip it
This crime we commit
Oh! What a shame

Some try to keep it alive
Deep down into it dive
But when the flame dies
Tears swell up in eyes
Even to each other lie
Oh! What a shame

It is in your hands entire
To cool or keep burning
your desires
Add wood to move its flames
higher
Why act a liar
Why be a crier
Oh! What a shame

Love is not to blame

Why give it names
When it is the mind
that plays games
We bloom it, we nip it
This crime we commit
Oh! What a shame

Had all loved
then love would have existed
Things would not appear
dead or twisted
We beings crave getting attached
While that love, tip toes
and gets detached
Oh! What a shame.

©Sunita Grover Raina
India.

ECHOED BY HIM

In the garden of hearts, love's flame does dance
A delicate game of fate and chance

We nurture it, we watch it grow
Yet often, it's the mind's winds that blow

Love bears no guilt for the tears we shed
Nor the tangled webs in which we're led

We strive to keep its fire burning bright
But sometimes, it dims in sorrow's night

It's within our grasp to fan the fire
Or let it dwindle, lost to desire

Why do we choose to deceive and feign?
Oh, what a shame, this cycle of pain

If all embraced love's tender embrace
Perhaps it wouldn't vanish without a trace

But we cling and crave, yet fear the bond
And love slips away, like grains of sand

Love is not to blame, we must refrain
From labeling it with guilt and shame

For in the end, it's our hearts that play
The games that lead love astray.

@Manu Adit. Dubai (UAE)

IN BITS AND PIECES I BROKE

So many pieces of mine
Remain frozen in time

Waiting on the roads I walked
Time with purpose surely them stalked

Rooted they stand like dazed dolls
Hoping to be woken by a call

To fulfill those pending dreams
Which they are hiding behind screens

But leaving them I walked ahead
They stood there, though breathing but dead

How do I them revive
Can I once again in the past dive

They are waiting on the roads I walked
Time with purpose surely them stalked

How can I leave them waiting
They are parts of me awaiting

Though they are stone statues lifeless
Will carry them along and turn them timeless.

©Sunita Grover Raina
India.

ECHOED BY HIM

In fragments and shards, I lay
Scattered through the years, astray

Each piece a memory, a part of me
Frozen in time, longing to be free

They linger on the paths I tread
Captured by time, where dreams have fled

Like silent statues, they yearn to awaken
Their whispers lost, their spirits shaken

But as I wander, forging ahead
They remain, silent and unsaid

How do I breathe life into the past
And free these fragments, bound so fast?

They wait along the roads I roam
Aching to find their way back home

Though now they seem lifeless and cold
I'll weave them into stories untold
For in fragments and pieces, I broke
Lies the power to mend and evoke

@Manu Adit
Dubai (UAE)

(POEM -4) Sunita Grover Raina & Manu Adithyan

DEATH TURNED LOVER

Death came knocking
On the door
Fell in love
Could not her ignore

Neither did he want
to let her be
Nor did he want her
to paradise see

Pretended to be
a part of this world
In order to be
with this girl

What could he do
but stay
Till he found
another way

But she knew
he was death
it was time
to leave her berth

Saw death too
had feelings
Not a devil he
as all believing

And she
fell in love too
Looked at him
with a different view

Told him
she is ready to go
No more will fear,
come to show

On her face,
as he lovingly cared
When death is a lover,
everything can be dared.

EVEN DEATH.

©Sunita Grover Raina
India.

ECHOED BY HIM

In the shadow's embrace
Love and death entwine

A tango of fate
A dance divine

She, the mortal
He, the eternal night

In their forbidden love
They find their light

Whispers of eternity
In her fleeting breath

His cold touch, tender
Defying life and death

In the stillness of time
They share a silent vow

A love so profound
It transcends the now

She embraces his chill
With fearless grace

In death's tender arms
She finds her resting place

An eternal romance
In life's final breath

For in the arms of death
They find love, undying, until death.

@Manu Adit
Dubai (UAE)

(POEM-5) Sunita Grover Raina & Manu Adithyan.

I AM TIME

With passing time my wounds did heal
Was it time or my inner zeal?

Time just flows and waits for none
It has no time for anyone

My inner self had given up
Who placed my feet in both stirrups

I am racing since and never stopped
Reins tightly held and never dropped

Where to I run, I do not know
Which path to choose, no one did show

I too shall pass and never pause
I too am time and with a cause

I want to see the end of time
I want to see the end of mine

If time lives on as an endless future
Somewhere in future, I will be sutured

History repeats itself they say
Then I too, with time, will come to stay.

@Sunita Grover Raina. India

ECHOED BY HIM

In the cosmic chronicle of time
my spirit weaves,
A dance of moments
where destiny cleaves

With each tick of the clock
my wounds find rest
Bound by time's caress
at nature's behest

Does time heal
or the fire within my soul?
An enigma woven in life's
timeless scroll

Time, the silent river
flows without a glance
Unmoved by mortal dreams
in its graceful dance

Who holds the reins of fate
my heart in strife?
In the endless race
the pulse of life

I gallop through the mists
with no path to claim
Lost in the labyrinth

seeking fortune's name

For time is but a phantom
a fleeting breath
I, too, am time
entwined in life and death

In the symphony of moments
I seek my chime
Yearning to glimpse
the end of time's paradigm

If time is endless
a river without shore
I'll be stitched in its fabric
forever more

They say history repeats
in endless array
So I, too, with time
shall find my destined way

In the grand tapestry of time
we all play a part
Entwined in its embrace
beating in every heart.

@Manu Adit
Dubai (UAE)

WILD FLOWER

I would rather be a mountain wild flower
Than a trapped pansy in a dandy penthouse
bower

My petals though small
Enthrals all
All bend to touch me
With love in their gaze see
Lovers frolic around in fun

In madness run
The penthouse beauties
Never were free
Either in rooms of glass houses

Or decorated in flower vases
Not even allowed to live their full stay
Then in a flick thrown away
While I get to see the loving smiles

Which, ever bloom on lips and in eyes
How carefully they move in the hills
So that steps do not accidently kill
My every birth a thrill.

©Sunita Grover Raina
India

ECHOED BY HIM

In the meadows wide and free I'd rather be
A wild flower dancing, wild and so carefree

My roots may not reach deep
But my spirit's awake, not asleep

I sway with the breeze, untouched by human hand
In nature's embrace, I proudly stand

Lovers find me in their secret retreat
Where passion and fervour joyfully meet

While in the city, trapped in gilded towers
Pansies wilt, deprived of nature's powers

Confined in glass and ornate vases
Their beauty fades in artificial spaces

But I, in the wild, bloom with every dawn
With every petal, a new life is born

Their steps avoid me, reverent and still
Preserving my essence, as if I were a thrill

So let me be the wild flower on the hill
Where freedom and beauty dance with skill.

@Manu Adit
Dubai (UAE)

(POEM-7) Sunita Grover Raina & Manu Adithyan.

THEN STARTS THE FUN

Be it a petal
or a feather
If I get one
then starts the fun

I keep blowing
and they keep going
Up, up in the air
They lose all fear

For safe they feel
flying around
Never will I let them
touch the ground

For I fly too
In the sky so blue
That feather is me
That petal is me

That is exactly how
them I see
The feeling of
sinking
Lulls me to sleep
The higher I fly

The slumber is deep

Be it a petal
or a feather
If I get one
then starts the fun.

©Sunita Grover Raina
India.

ECHOED BY HIM

Amidst the gentle breeze
A petal or feather at ease
In my hand they find their way
And then begins a dance so gay

I set them free, watch them soar
Up, up in the sky they explore
Their worries vanish, all fears unfurl
As they embrace the boundless world

I, too, take flight, with them I roam
In the vast, cerulean dome
For in that feather, in that petal light
I see reflections of my own flight

As I ascend, the earth grows small
And in this ascent, I heed the call
The warmth of sinking bids me to sleep
In the embrace of skies so deep

Be it a petal or a feather
In their flight, we are together
For when I set just one of them free
Then starts the fun, and I am wild and free.

@Manu Adit
Dubai (UAE)

(POEM-8) Sunita Grover Raina & Manu Adithyan.

WEAR ME

Make my fragrance
the perfume you wear
I will bottle myself up
for you

The only way I ensure
to be with you dear
This I want,
is my wish true

Sniff me in whiffs
dab on handkerchiefs
Or touch me
on the throbbing
pulse behind your ears

I will hide in your hair
And lovingly peer
In your eyes
While you unaware
Of my presence
In the essence
Has entwined you
Forever

You will live your births
In which ever earths
Does not matter dear
I will be with you there.

©Sunita Grover Raina
India

35

ECHOED BY HIM

Embrace my essence
let it be your cloak
A scent of memories
in whispers bespoke

I'll bottle my love
for you to unfurl
A timeless connection
through each precious twirl

In fragrant whispers
I'll linger near
A touch of my soul
to calm every fear

Dab me on evenings
when the world seems unkind
Let my love be the solace
that you seek and find.

Feel me in the rhythm
of your pulse's soft beat
A comforting presence
in moments bittersweet

In the tangle of your locks
I'll find my repose

Gazing through your eyes
where my devotion flows

Unseen yet felt
in the depths of your core
My love will surround you
Forever more.

Across countless lifetimes
in lands near and far
I'll be by your side
like a guiding star

So wear me, dear friend
as time dances on
In the symphony of life
may my love be drawn

With each breath you take
in the joys that you share
Know that my spirit
will always be there.

@Manu Adit
Dubai (UAE)

(POEM-9) Sunita Grover Raina & Manu Adithyan.

FREE I AM

If I am singing
I am surely caring
For my soul
Which was quiet
within

Who says I sinned
Just self was tinned
I let it out
With a can opener
Was a sojourner

And no wonder
My songs leaked out
And killed the
Drought

Singing I am
Curing I am
From liars goddamn.

©Sunita Grover Raina
India.

ECHOED BY HIM

In the depths of my being, a melody stirs
A response to your song, my spirit's true words

Unshackled and free, I am embracing my truth
Unveiling the layers, reclaiming my youth

Once hidden within, my soul now takes flight
No longer confined, no longer contrite

With each note that escapes, a burden is shed
A symphony of healing, where falsehoods are
bled

So I sing with conviction, I sing with resolve
Untangling the lies, my spirit evolves

From the chains of deceit, I am breaking away
Revelling in freedom, with each note I play

No longer bound by the whispers of shame
I reclaim my power, I stake my claim

In the echoes of truth, I find my release
Embracing my essence, my soul finds its peace.

@Manu Adit
Dubai (UAE)

(POEM-10) Sunita Grover Raina & Manu Adithyan.

AM I GUILTY

I could have loved better
More freely more dearly
Had not the guilt collared me

Half of me said to love is not a crime
The other half said it is just a matter of time

Were my halves truly on my side?
Or they indirectly tried

To tighten the collar of guilt around my neck
Did the meaning of love change

When I stretched my wings
Increased the range

I had loved
Still love
And will love again

Then why this guilt
within me built

When love itself flew away
Showed me a new way

And I did sway

What do I suffer from,
what is this guilt about
At times, love's meaning I doubt

Why can't I live and think like others
All my life I ran after my thoughts
hither and thither.

©Sunita Grover Raina
India.

ECHOED BY HIM

Am I guilty for the love I didn't give?
Could I have loved more freely and truly live?

Guilt, a collar tight around my beating heart,
Torn between love's pull and the fear to depart.

Half of me yearning for love's pure embrace
The other half caged in a suffocating space

Entwined by doubt, by the weight of my own
soul
Caught in a web of guilt, I struggle to feel whole.

Did my halves conspire to shackle my desire?
Or did love's own nature ignite this inner fire

I have loved, I love, and will love once more
Yet this burden of guilt, what purpose does it
store?

As love slips away, showing me a different view
I question the meaning, wondering if it's true

Why does this guilt linger, causing me to doubt
As I chase after thoughts, within and without?

Why can't I break free, like others who roam

Embracing love's journey, finding a place called
home?

Let me unravel this guilt, let my spirit fly
For in love's boundless realm, I'll spread my
wings and touch the sky.

@Manu Adit
Dubai (UAE)

(POEM-11) Sunita Grover Raina & Manu Adithyan.

WORRIES

Thinking about your worries
won't get you anywhere

Just more and more wrinkles will appear,
here and there

If you can get rid of them
Then do it fast
Or they will slowly eat you
and you won't last

If you believe in destiny
then why think of worries
as an enemy

Let them in corner be
and you move ahead
Get their thoughts
out of your head
With time they too
will be dead

You torture yourself
and you torture your soul
Those worries will surely

to disturb you, troll

Master the trick that worrying thoughts
don't appear
Then see the magic how quickly
they disappear

Have you seen the face of a dead body
How young it looks, as worries no longer
it embodies

Finally death will do it
but you can do it too
Kill them before they trap
and kill you.

©Sunita Grover Raina
India.

ECHOED BY HIM

Worries can't be merry but they
dance with you
whisper you tales of fear and woe
Plant their seeds for doubts to grow

Like vultures circling in the sky
They prey upon the weakened sigh

With every step, they weigh you down
Until your spirit starts to drown

But worry, dear, won't save the day
Nor guide you through the dark dismay

It steals the joy from present time,
And chains the heart with silent crime.

So cast them off, let worries flee
And set your troubled spirit free

Embrace the now, let fears depart
And feel the lightness in your heart

For life is brief, and time won't stall
So don't let worries claim it all

Release their grip, reclaim your fate
And find the peace that can't abate

In every breath, in every sigh
Let worries fade and pass on by

Embrace the dawn, let troubles go
And feel the weight of worry's woe

For in the end, when all is said
It's love and joy that you should wed

So set your worries free to roam,
And find the peace that leads you home.

@Manu Adit
Dubai (UAE)

(POEM-12) Sunita Grover Raina & Manu Adithyan.

MISFIT

I always see myself
a misfit
I understand all
When it comes to me
they stall

They become liars
Together conspire
Strange character acquire

Fed up am I now
Convince myself somehow

Let them be
When they cannot see

Alone you came
Alone you be

Alone we leave
is our destiny

It is just the phase
between birth and death
Which we need to unearth

48

You did it
That is why you are a misfit.

©Sunita Grover Raina
India.

ECHOED BY HIM (A)

(Here is an opposite compilation)

Amidst the crowd, you feel alone
A misfit in this world, unknown.

But listen close, to these words I say
You're unique, in your own way

When others falter, and turn away
Don't lose heart, or let dismay hold sway

Their lies and conspiring, leave you in doubt
But believe in yourself, don't count yourself out

Embrace your strangeness, it's a gift, you see
A mark of individuality

Let them be, if they cannot perceive
The beauty in you, they fail to believe

Alone you came, and alone you'll be
But in that solitude, you're truly free

For in the end, we all depart
Alone, yet connected, by the beating heart

The path you walk is yours to tread
From birth to death, where life is led

The phase you're in, misunderstood a bit
But remember this, you're more than a misfit

So stand tall, embrace your unique light
Shine brightly through the darkest night

You've braved the storm, you don't submit
For in your difference, you're truly exquisite.

@Manu Adit
Dubai (UAE)

ECHOED BY HIM (B)

You grasp your purpose with clarity
and radiate with sincerity

Trust your words, we seek your light
In your presence, things feel right

Content and at peace, you stand tall
Embracing your role, you heed the call

Let them come, let them see
The strength that resides within you

Connected with all, yet firmly in place
You belong, you thrive in life's embrace

In the dance of existence, you find your worth
Navigating the journey from birth to rebirth

You did it, you found your place
That's why you're not a misfit, but a perfect fit in
life's embrace.

@Manu Adit
Dubai (UAE)

(POEM-13) Sunita Grover Raina & Manu Adithyan.

DEW DROP

Hey dew drop stop sticking to the leaf
Enough of your plans to attract

You think you are a pearl
You are worse than a wooden burl

In a second I can expose your reality
Slight jerk on the leaf will prove the actuality

Forever your presence will vanish
Your reputation I can tarnish

It is that leaf that allows that adherence
And along with light gives you the pearly
appearance

Enjoy your short glory which sun allows
Before he into oblivion, sets your destination
A fake you are, that gives temporary excitement

And when you disappear
No one actually cares

For they have the showy ones at home
To dazzle other's eyes.

©Sunita Grover Raina
India

ECHOED BY HIM

In the morning sun's gentle embrace
A dew drop clings to a leaf's grace

Glistening like a precious gem
Yet fleeting, just a tiny emblem

But oh, dew drop, do you not see
Your beauty is but a transient spree

For with a touch, your illusion breaks
Leaving behind no trace of lakes

You dance upon the leaf so fair
But in the end, you'll vanish into thin air

A mere mirage, a passing delight
Gone with the day, out of sight

Your allure is but a fleeting game
A transient joy, a moment's claim

Yet know this, dear dew drop, before you go
In your brief existence, you put on quite a show

So shimmer and shine, while you may
For in your brief life, you have your say

But remember, dear dew, in the grand design
Ephemeral beauty, the heart will enshrine.

@Sunita Grover Raina
India

(POEM-14) Sunita Grover Raina & Manu Adithyan.

A ROMANCER

What is my search I wish I really knew
What is it, that I want from the day I really grew

I want something this much I truly know
Like waves I reach the shore

and then pulled back to something show
Like a Yo Yo, I am made to roll up and down

Then left dangling like a hanging circus clown
Spun like a spinning top on many a palm

They are happy, but my ins merge with the outs

At times made to kick pebbles on the road
At times made to bathe in rain, maybe to goad

I do whatever I feel like or made by destiny to do
But keep my search on and then sit down to
review

Seems like my research and search will never
end

All this will remain here and me to him, will
death send

A total failure who could not get any of her
answers
Did I waste my life, Nay! Ever a life romancer.

©Sunita Grover Raina
India.

ECHOED BY HIM

What is this quest, this burning desire
Unseen yet felt, like a soul on fire

What do I seek, from the morn of my birth
In the endless skies, and the boundless earth

I yearn for something, this much is clear
Like the tides to the moon, drawn near yet far

I touch the sands of the elusive shore
Then swept away, to search some more

A pendulum's motion, this life I lead
Swinging back and forth, by fate's decree

I am but a jester in life's grand play
Spinning in circles, day after day

Tossed and turned like a leaf in the wind
In the hands of fate, to their whims pinned

They laugh, they cheer, but deep inside
My essence blurs, where does it reside

I've kicked the stones, felt the rain's cold kiss
Chasing fleeting moments of ephemeral bliss

I've danced with destiny, played its cruel game
Yet the hunger persists, ever the same

This journey, this search, seems without an end
The mysteries of life, refusing to bend

All will stay behind, when death makes its call
Just me and my questions, that's all

A failure, you say? Ah, but you're wrong
In this dance with life, I've found my song

Not a wasted moment, not a wasted chance
I am, and will always be, life's eternal romancer.

@Manu Adit
Dubai (UAE)

(POEM-15) Sunita Grover Raina & Manu Adithyan.

FIX BROKEN HEARTS

A broken heart
is hard to fix
In waves of doubt
its heart beat ticks

Like a frightened tortoise
in its shell
Love hides within such hearts
and dwells

You can see it peeping
through the eyes
With other hearts
to touch it tries

To fix a broken heart
fully
Win its trust
Dutifully

Trust is first needed
then love
For it is now
a wounded dove

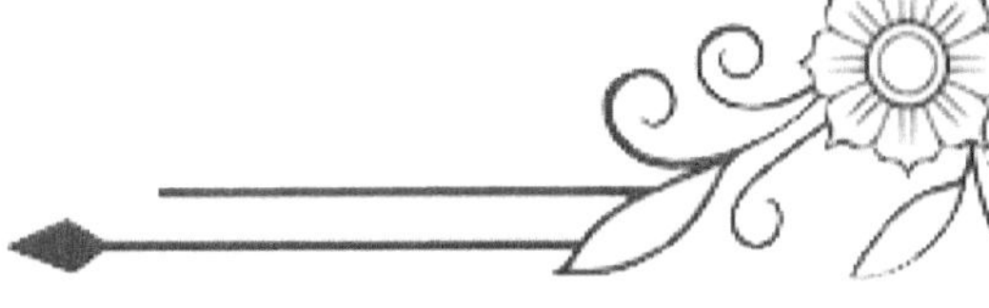

Keep patience,
let it slowly near
Every step it takes,
is loaded with fear

Do not lecture,
do not haste
Let not your effort,
go to waste

When this trust,
within it comes
Now sprinkle love,
in little sums

Do not suffocate,
with any excess
Let it consume
and let it access

Slowly, will come
and rest on you
Try to bask,
in your loving hue

Love it now,
go slow and steady
Broken heart,

now addicted and heady

It is fixed,
God made it happen
Keep loving it,
never let it sadden.

©Sunita Grover Raina
India

ECHOED BY HIM

A shattered soul, a wounded core
In silent agony, it longs for more

Like a fragile sparrow, it seeks to mend
With tender care, and love to lend

You glimpse its yearning, in tear-streaked eyes
Aching for solace, beneath darkened skies

To heal a shattered soul, requires patience
profound
Rebuilding trust, on fragile ground

Trust must bloom, before love's embrace
For it's a fragile dance, in this sacred space

Be not hasty, nor overly keen
Let love unfold, like a gentle stream

With cautious steps, it nears your side
Every move laden, with fears to confide

Refrain from lectures, and rushing ways
Let love's gentle touch, guide the mending days

As trust takes root, in the wounded heart's core
Sprinkle love's essence, like never before

Avoid suffocation, with love's excess
Allow it to breathe, and freely express

In time, it finds refuge, within your caring
embrace
Let it bask in love's warmth, in its newfound
place

Love it tenderly, with patience and grace
The shattered soul, now finds its place

Slowly, it heals, in a steady embrace
Mended by love, in a sacred space

It is whole once more, a miracle woven
Cherish it always, in love unbroken.

@Manu Adit
Dubai (UAE)

(POEM-16) Sunita Grover Raina & Manu Adithyan.

SOUND OF SILENCE

In the stillness of the hills
In the silence of the hills

Did you see the waltzing stream
slithering down to meet you?

Her enticing hum ever remaining
in my conscience and
resonating in my dreams

As a back ground music
being played again and again.
Only to surface when nothing remains

Did you see your entire self
vibrating along with her

The need and feel of
everything around diminishing

The near and far merging to become one
Under the moon and under the sun
Her hum
the sound of silence

Did you see that it does not matter
if you are still sitting here
and the stream is there

You could be with her
and she with you
at the same instance

What difference does it make
For you could even be her
What time? Which space?
Whoosh!
Only the Sound of Silence

©Sunita Grover Raina
India.

ECHOED BY HIM

In the hush of the hills so grand
In the quiet of the hills so grand

Do you feel the gentle breeze
whispering secrets in your ear

Its tender touch lingering in the depths of your
soul
and dancing in your dreams

Like a timeless melody playing over and over
Only to resurface when all else fades

Do you feel your whole being swaying to its
rhythm
The clamour of the world fading into obscurity

The close and the distant converging
Beneath the stars,

Beneath the sun
Its murmur the sound of silence

Do you perceive that it matters not if you sit
here
and the breeze is there

You could be within it

and it within you at this very moment

What significance does it hold
For you could even be it

What time? What space? Whoosh!
Only the Sound of Silence

In the stillness, in the silence
We find our true essence

In the sound of silence
We discover our connectedness

@Manu Adit
Dubai (UAE)

(POEM-17) Sunita Grover Raina & Manu Adithyan.

WHERE DO I HIDE

I was staring at the sky
Sitting under a tree
Hidden by its boughs
In the dead of night
Thinking no one could see me

The tears in my eyes
The beats of my heart
Racing up and down
With my choking thoughts
Thinking no one could see me

How would I know
The moon was observing
The stars were wondering
Ways to appease me, while I
Thinking no one could see me

The pain put me to sleep
The cold curled me in weep
Eyes shut, I shut off world
For dreams to take care of me

Thinking no one could see me

Woke up with stars in my eyes
Boughs wrapped around me
A quilt of green soft leaves
My face now a lovely moon
Loved by those who could see me

©Sunita Grover Raina
India

ECHOED BY HIM

In the shadows of the night
Where do I hide, you ask
Beneath the weight of heavy thoughts
I seek a refuge, a tranquil mask

I rest beneath the ancient oak
Its branches cradle my despair
While tears may fall, unseen by all
The moon and stars, they're aware

Their silent whispers touch my soul
As I surrender to the night
In the embrace of nature's arms
I find solace, a guiding light

As sleep descends, the pain recedes
A tender peace begins to grow
In dreams, I'm free from earthly binds
In dreams, my spirit starts to glow

Awakening to the morning dew
I find myself adorned in grace
The tree, my shelter, stood by me
In its embrace, I've found my place.

@Manu Adit
Dubai (UAE)

(POEM-18) Sunita Grover Raina & Manu Adithyan.

LOVING SPIRIT AROUND ME

Bet you have never seen a spirit
But I know a spirit who loves me
Though I have never seen his presence
He is always there around me

Funny I never fear his movement
In the big home where I reside in
He guards my every step I take
Breathing warm sighs around me

At times I feel he touched my hair
My hands my cheeks my rolling tears
My lips by little wisps of air
Dancing his soul around me

I wonder will he show his form
Is it possible for him to don
A physical look which I could see
But only a fragrance around me

What a wonderful feeling I do get
I wait patiently for him to act
My extra sensory perceptions set
Perceiving his love around me

©Sunita Grover Raina
India

71

ECHOED BY HIM

Invisible threads of love and care
Envelop me in a tender embrace
A spirit's presence, unseen yet felt
Guiding, guarding, with gentle grace

Unseen hands that brush my hair
And wipe away my silent tears
Whispers of comfort in the air
A loving spirit, calming fears

In the quiet moments,
I sense your nearness
A fragrance of love, a touch so light
Though formless, your essence is clear

A presence that fills my heart with delight
I long to catch a glimpse, to behold
This spirit's form, your radiant glow
But perhaps your love is meant to unfold

As a fragrance, a whisper, that I know
So I'll cherish this bond, this ethereal tie
And with open heart, I'll patiently wait
For the spirit's love will never die

A comforting presence, my loving fate.

@Manu Adit
Dubai (UAE)

(POEM-19) Sunita Grover Raina & Manu Adithyan.

DEAR ALL CAN'T BE SAID

In every madness of mine
A little bit of my love shines
You could not it, ever see
As you never had time to love me
Dear all can't be said

Had you paid attention
To my volatile tantrums
You could have read them
There was no need to condemn
Dear all can't be said

This madness had love within
You just needed to rip this coating thin
There was a heaven waiting
Love so innocent and satiating
Dear all can't be said

My madness increased
Your nearness decreased
You said this was living hell
And walked out so well
Dear all can't be said

But you entered into wilderness
My life an unsolved emptiness
All I needed were frequent hugs

Here and there some playful tugs
Dear all can't be said

A little bit of loving touch
Even if it was an angry clutch
When my madness was at the peak
It would have done the magical trick
Dear all can't be said

But all you saw was the madness
Not the love and hidden sadness
The acute craving and the distress
Your dead heart could never guess
Dear all can't be said

You thought about it with head
Viewed me as an unbuttered bread
But the adamant ass that I am
Kept knocking you like a wild Ram
Dear all can't be said

For I wanted you to read me right
Draw out the curtains, let in bright light
Clear your visions of the wrong you sight
Kept hope burning, one day you might.
Dear all can't be said

©Sunita Grover Raina
India

ECHOED BY HIM

In every moment of my madness
A spark of love quietly dances
Yet you failed to perceive its light
For you never had the time to hold me tight
Dear all can't be said

If only you had glimpsed the signs
In my tempestuous, turbulent lines
You might have understood without blame
There was no need for scorn or shame
Dear all can't be said

Within my madness, love did reside
Yearning for you to see it, to guide
Towards a place of innocent bliss
Where love's pure touch you would not miss
Dear all can't be said

As my madness grew, your closeness waned
You deemed it a living hell, and refrained
Walking away with graceful ease
Leaving my heart in desperate pleas
Dear all can't be said

Into the wilds of emptiness I fell
Yearning for your touch, a spell
Of frequent hugs and playful tugs

To soothe my soul that yearns and tugs
Dear all can't be said

A touch of love, even in anger's grasp
Amidst my madness, a love that lasts
It could have worked its magic deep
Yet you only saw the madness, not the love to
keep
Dear all can't be said

You pondered with logic in your head
Seeing me as an untouched loaf of bread
Yet failed to glimpse the depth within
The anguish, the yearning, the love so thin
Dear all can't be said

But in my heart, the love remains
Despite your departure, it sustains
For in my madness, a love so true
Endures the pain, still reaching for you
Dear all can't be said

So here I stand, an adamant soul
With love and madness, my heart's true goal
For in the chaos, love does reside
Dear all, within the madness, love can't hide.

@Manu Adit
Dubai (UAE)

(POEM-20) Sunita Grover Raina & Manu Adithyan.

WINGS OF SOUL

They came flying when my doors opened
Then it was my voice they followed
My silent tip toeing too they sensed
Maybe my breaths also they hear

They sense my arrival and come flapping
Happy kissing, coo cooing and flapping
Thrilled are they using their wings for clapping
What when the pyre burns me

I am sure my soul they will see
One or two will surely wait on my Neem tree
I too will come to greet
For my soul will have wings so free

They talk about unconditional love
and similar things
I found humans the most treacherous beings
Ever changing colours in every dealing
Wings they clip with no feelings.

©Sunita Grover Raina
India

ECHOED BY HIM

In the stillness of the night, they soar
Guided by the whispers of my soul
Wings of ethereal grace, they explore
Boundless love, their eternal role

With tender touch, they alight on my spirit
Their presence, a symphony of devotion
In their eyes, I see infinite merit
A dance of love, a timeless emotion

When my earthly tether fades to dust
Will they linger, in the shadows and light
Will they wait, with unwavering trust,
To guide my soul, through the endless night

For in their embrace, I find solace
Beyond the realm of human artifice
In their wings, I see boundless grace
An undying love, beyond any vice

So let the world change and deceive
Let human hearts falter and wane
For in the wings of love, I believe
Eternal freedom, an unbreakable chain.

@Manu Adit
Dubai (UAE)

(POEM-21) Sunita Grover Raina & Manu Adithyan.

SEVEN LIFETIMES!

There go lovers with love filled eyes
For what do you cry
Hey! Let the tears dry

Love for you takes shape in dreams
In reality, yes different it seems

How many steps together could you walk
Terms and conditions appeared in every talk

Do you really know what love actually is
Can you sacrifice everything for this

What a joke! You felt, is it not
You were bothered about what could be got

Love is not a business deal
Neither is it a five course meal

It is a promise made by both
It is a lifelong oath

Seven rounds around the fire made
A bond for seven lifetimes arrayed

Could you even walk seven steps honestly
Ask your heart, it will reply, hardly

There go lovers with love filled eyes
For what do you cry
Hey! Let the tears dry.

©Sunita Grover Raina
India.

ECHOED BY HIM

In the realm of love, a journey untold
Heartbeats entwined, a story unfolds

Do you fathom what love truly means
Beyond the facade, beneath the scenes

Not a contract penned in ink and gold
Nor a prize to grasp, a tale to be told

Love is not a mere transaction's art
Nor a fleeting feast, a transient part

It's a sacred vow, a binding tie
A dance of souls under the open sky

Seven lifetimes, a bond of timeless grace
Can you tread seven steps, embrace and face

The depth of love, its uncharted quest
A journey of souls, a lifelong zest

So let the tears dry, for love is near
In whispered vows, in every heartfelt tear

There go lovers with love-filled eyes
For what do you cry, let the fears subside.

@Manu Adit
Dubai (UAE)

(POEM-22) Sunita Grover Raina & Manu Adithyan.

A GOLDEN HALO

You are running from life
You fear to face strife
How will you get god

He hides in things he gives
But ever, you miss this
How will you get god

You run after nice things
But these are distracting flings
How will you get god

Just go, just flow
Be it flowers, be it blows
On every path will he show
A golden halo.

©Sunita Grover Raina
India.

ECHOED BY HIM

On every path you roam
Seeking light to call your own

Golden halos in the air
Whispering secrets, beyond compare

In the flowers, in the blows
God's presence softly glows

Embrace the journey, let it unfold
A golden halo, a tale untold

Fear not the strife, nor the chase
For within you, there's a sacred space

Where love and truth intertwine
A golden halo, forever divine

Let go of distractions, let go of fear
For in surrender, the divine is near

Embrace the moment, let your spirit grow
A golden halo, within and below.

@Manu Adit
Dubai (UAE)

(POEM-23) Sunita Grover Raina & Manu Adithyan.

MY SWEETHEART SUN

Why sneak under my door
Are you still not sure
North or South
East or West
You are the king
Every life sings
Without you none can survive
Even the ocean fearfully lets you dive
Keeping your bed cool so that you rise
With the majestic radiance you uprise
We have been ever playing this game
of hide and seek
But your rays reach
every nook and creek
And this is my home
where you sneak to hide
And I waiting to grab you
and confide
That seek me out ever
And forever
Oh Light! That wakes and
never ceases to bless
Every Universe
My every verse.

©Sunita Grover Raina 2023
India.

ECHOED BY HIM

Underneath the cosmic dance of stars so grand
A soulful plea, a heart's demand

My dearest friend, the sweet and gentle Sun
Your warmth and light, our lives have spun

Your radiant embrace, a daily gift so true
From dawn's first blush to the evening's adieu

In every corner, in every hidden space
Your touch, your grace, on every face

A game of light and shadow, we endlessly play
Seeking, yearning, for your golden ray

Oh celestial guide, keeper of time
In your luminous journey, we find our rhyme

So hear my plea, as the new year starts anew
Shine on, dear Sun, in skies so blue

Illuminate our days, with your timeless art
And forever bless, every beating heart.

@Manu Adit
Dubai (UAE)

(POEM-24) Sunita Grover Raina & Manu Adithyan.

EYES

Eyes that have the ocean within
Eyes that have never sinned

Eyes full of innocence
Eyes not knowing insolence

Eyes that might be dreaming
Eyes ever redeeming

Eyes that caught my eye
Eyes that never lie

Eyes which make me dream
Eyes that never schemed

Eyes that I think about
Eyes divine they, no doubt

Eyes of the blind are they
Eyes that can't see but have a lot to say

Eyes without light, do you dream too?
Wish my eyes could, your dreams view.

©Sunita Grover Raina
India.

ECHOED BY HIM

In the depths of darkness, where light cannot
reach
Resides a world of dreams, an unspoken speech

Eyes that know not the colours of day
Yet paint vivid pictures in their own unique way

Eyes closed to the sight of the waking hour
But open wide to the realms of inner power

Eyes that mirror the depth of the soul
Reflecting emotions that words cannot control

Eyes that see not the external gleam
Yet sparkle with visions that dance in a dream

Eyes of the blind, tell me what you perceive
In the silent whispers that your dreams weave

Eyes that inspire, though they cannot see
Reveal the beauty of a world yet to be

@Manu Adit
Dubai (UAE)

(POEM-25) Sunita Grover Raina & Manu Adithyan.

Down Feathers

Was it dew drops, snow flakes
or splashes from the lake

Was it rain drops or rose petals
Surely, something on me fell

Hey! Look up
then things will be clear
Their down feathers they share

Your pigeons dear
Are turning themselves bare

Yes, very cold it is
Their way of protecting is this

This warmth how could I miss
Every plume that touched
was a warm kiss

There are so many things more beautiful
But to many are not noticeable

Blessed I am, blessings never stopped
It was love soaked plumes
they dropped

Droppings at times fell on me too
*That too as a sign of luck I view.

©Sunita Grover Raina
India.

• In India bird droppings on head and shoulders
is considered a sign of good fortune coming your
way.

ECHOED BY HIM

In a world of whispers and whispers of the world
Feathers fall, stories untold, unfurl

Was it whispers of the wind, or secrets from the
sky
Softly, gently, they descended by

Look up, dear friend, and the truth will appear
For the down feathers they share, hold secrets
dear

Your pigeons, they shed in the cold wintry air
Their sacrifice, a testament, beyond compare

In their downy embrace, warmth is found
Every plume that touched, a love profound

So many marvels, unnoticed they remain
Yet love-soaked plumes, they soothe the pain

Blessed we are, as the world spins and wept
For the love-soaked plumes, they softly crept

Droppings of luck, they too fell on me
A sign of fortune, a blessing to see

In the dance of feathers, a tale is spun
Of love and luck, beneath the morning sun.

@Manu Adit
Dubai (UAE)

(POEM-26) Sunita Grover Raina & Manu Adithyan.

PETALS THAT WHISTLED

My friends of school days came to mind
How difficult are they now to find

The cement blocks have killed them all
Last fifty years I searched and called

The chill in the wind made me to whistle
Suddenly remembered the poppy thistle

How I plucked the yellow petals
Blew tunes, matching boiling kettles

Such little things gave me pleasure
Took some home to blow in leisure

Though pricked I was with deadly thorns
This game went on, this game went on

Wonder if any match my feelings
I search those poppies for my wound's healing

My friends of school days came to mind
How difficult are they now to find.

©Sunita Grover Raina
India.

From net
SATYANASHI (HINDI NAME) FOR
MEXICAN POPPIES

ECHOED BY HIM

In the garden of memories, I wander alone
Seeking the friends of my youth, now overgrown

Concrete and steel have swallowed their laughter
Leaving me to chase echoes ever after

Yet in the whispering wind, a melody unfurls
Recalling the poppy's dance, its petals in whirls

I plucked them one by one, like golden notes of
song
A symphony of innocence to which I belonged

Their fragrant breath mingled with my joy
As I blew tunes, a carefree girl

Tiny treasures in my palm, delicate and bright
Bringing solace in the stillness of the night

Despite the thorns that drew blood from my skin
I reveled in the music, the dance, the grin

Now I wonder, in fields far and wide
If those poppies still bloom, in love and pride

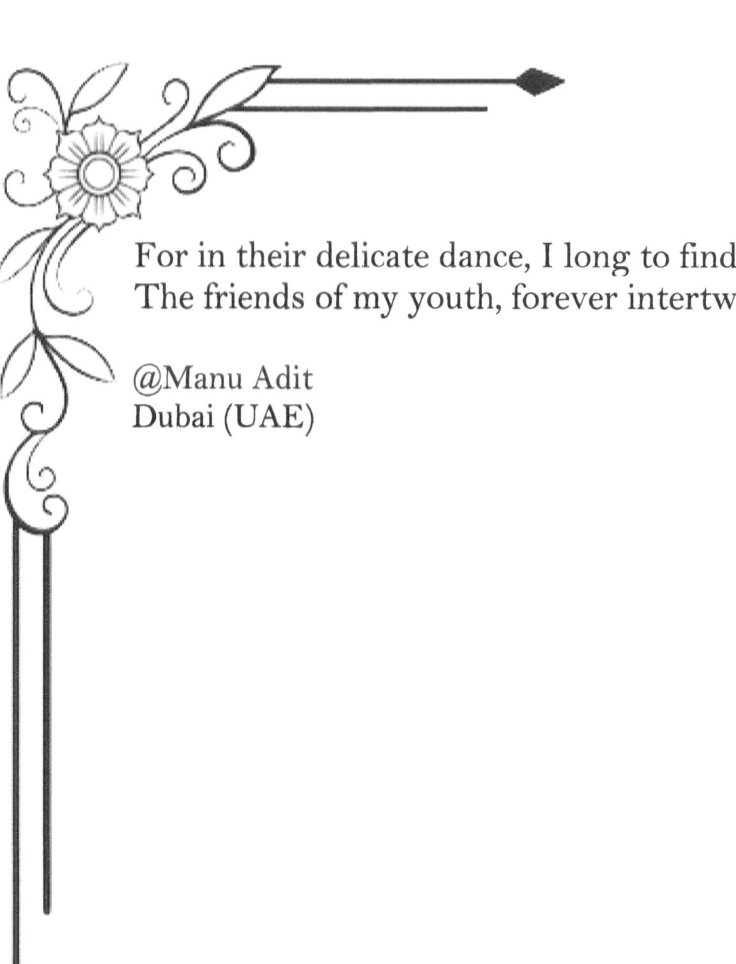

For in their delicate dance, I long to find
The friends of my youth, forever intertwined.

@Manu Adit
Dubai (UAE)

(POEM-27) Sunita Grover Raina & Manu Adithyan.

MY POEMS ARE SUNG

Today those hundreds kissed and went
My cooing friends which God has sent

Never did I lonely feel
All my time my friends did steal

Never was I a great talker
But always a good observer

Communicate I can with all
When heart is pulled and love does call

Those flapping wings around my whole
Touch me deep, they touch my soul

Blessed I am, blessed with lovely friends
They make me young, they make me young

In their *goottar gooing
In their love filled cooing
My poems are sung.

©Sunita Grover Raina
India.

*goottar gooing----sound of music,
the sound of pigeons.

ECHOED BY HIM

In the hush of twilight's gentle glow,
Where whispers of wings through the air do flow

A chorus of avian hearts takes flight
Their melodies weave through the fleeting night

Each flutter and coo, a tender embrace
Filling the void, leaving no empty space

Their presence a balm to soothe and mend
A bond unbroken, a love without end

In silent moments, they touch my core
Their feathered grace, a beauty to adore

For in their song, I find my own voice
A symphony born, a reason to rejoice

Blessed am I, with friends so dear
Who make me young, dispelling every fear

In their gentle murmurs, my spirit is sprung
In their love-filled cooing, my poems are sung.

@Manu Adit
Dubai (UAE)

(POEM-28) Sunita Grover Raina & Manu Adithyan.

COME

Let misfortune chase me
I will never let it catch me
Come on chase I am a sprinter too

Let life place as many obstacles
I will never topple
Come arrange them
I am a hurdler too

Let death come to embrace
I will not shy away
Come hug me
I am a lover too.

©Sunita Grover Raina
India.

ECHOED BY HIM

In the dance of fate,
let misfortune pursue

Yet never shall it grasp this spirit free
Come, chase me

with your dark and stormy hue
For I am swifter than the wind, you see

Life, lay your obstacles before my path
I'll leap and conquer, never to succumb

Come, place them high, a daunting aftermath
For I'm a hurdler, strong and never numb

And when the final call of death draws near
I'll welcome it with open arms, not fear

Come, embrace me, for I am unafraid
A lover of the life I've lived and bade.

@Manu Adit
Dubai (UAE)

(POEM-29) Sunita Grover Raina & Manu Adithyan.

WISH I HAD LOVED MORE

Love at least, lets you,
get addicted to live
Why not freely, to each other, love give

I see them all tired, sad and sighing
Life is tough, when with each other, all are vying

Years fly off by time's gale,
not knowing doing what
I too now at this age, continuously this, think
about

What was I chasing, what was my this need
Destiny surely did it and it was not my greed

For I am still the same though with less
welcomed worries
Wish I had loved more to tell more of those love
stories

For love was then too but I was running for
wine
Worried that all could with it happily dine

But did I need so much that it seems now a load
Wish I had loved more and walked on love roads

Name and fame looks now just a useless game
My mad heart is yelling, how do I it tame

Nothing is more important than loving this life
Wish I had loved more and to love had obliged

How many years I lost not listening to my heart
I did everything that made love, within me
depart

Now it smiles and says what a crazy fool you
were
Better late than never, run into my arms dear

It has grasped me so tight, feel in heaven I am
This bond will not break even if I, day and night
be damned

Soaking in love, I am soaked to the brim
Wish I had loved more and sung then too, love
hymns.

©Sunita Grover Raina
India.

ECHOED BY HIM

Oh, the weight of time's relentless flight
Leaving me with thoughts to ponder in the night

Regrets and wishes swirling in my mind
A longing for the love I left behind

Love, the potion that addicts the soul
Why did I hesitate to let my heart be whole

I see weary faces, burdened by life's race
Competing for love, caught in its frenzied chase

Years slip away, like leaves in the wind,
Leaving me pondering, searching deep within

 What was I chasing, what did I truly need
Destiny's hand guided, it was not my greed

Still, I carry the same heart, with lesser woes
Wishing I had loved more, and let my spirit
glow

Love was present then, but I pursued other
wine
Fearing it would diminish, fearing it wasn't
mine

Did I truly need all that I sought to amass
Now it feels like a burden, a heavy, weighty mass

I yearn for the paths where love brightly glowed
Wishing I had loved more, and along love's
roads strolled

Name and fame, a hollow, fleeting game
My heart cries out, how do I quell its flame

Nothing surpasses the importance of embracing
this life
Wishing I had loved more, and embraced love's
sweet strife

How many years slipped by, deaf to my heart's
song
I let love slip away, thinking I was strong

Now it chuckles and whispers, "Foolish one,
come near
It's never too late, love is waiting, have no fear.

@Manu Adit
Dubai (UAE)

(POEM-30) Sunita Grover Raina & Manu Adithyan.

I SURVIVED

It is the smile that turns me beautiful
It shed all the dead cuticle

For myself had long ago died
Never could dare and ever had shied

Now I am alive
Into smiles I dive
See I survived

Who can dare to steal them
Or dare to condemn

I smile at you
I truly do

Tissues had died
For they had lied

Now I am alive
Into smiles I dive
See I survived.

©Sunita Grover Raina
India.

ECHOED BY HIM

In the wake of pain and strife, I stand
A survivor, forged through fire and sand

No longer shackled by the weight of despair
Rising from the ashes, beyond all compare

My spirit, once shrouded in darkness and gloom
Now blossoms like a rose in full bloom

For I have found the strength to revive
And in the radiance of my smile, I thrive

Gone are the days of silent, hidden tears
Replaced by laughter that conquers fears

No thief can pilfer this newfound delight
Nor can any soul cast shadows on my light

I smile, not to deceive, nor to pretend
But to celebrate the wounds
that chose to mend

For in the depths of my soul, true freedom's
derived
In the echo of my laughter, behold, I survived.

@Manu Adit
Dubai (UAE)

FLIGHT

I am still sitting on a swing
My moods once again has taken wings

A backward thrust needed to make me fly
For some time I rise in the sky

Only to be pulled down easily
And my feet touches the ground of reality

If your wings you yourself clip
From the swing's seat you yourself flip

Temporary are these pleasures
Pain grips in immense measures

The tears slide down, are real
But the smile a temporary bail

I pay myself to come out of the mess
To change the prisoner's dress

Still the false is appreciated
Yes at times the reality alleviated

This too not liked by some around
Intensity of thrust decreasing on ground

My flight gets clipped
They love getting my wings ripped

Now hundreds of wings around
Are flapping their wings to my sounds

The sound of my songs on love
Are carried by my precious doves

Though now I sit still on my swing
Great pleasure this stillness brings

You can still fly
And touch the sky.

©Sunita Grover Raina
 India.

ECHOED BY HIM

Upon the swing, I find my seat
Yearning for a flight so sweet

My soul desires to soar on high
Yet grounded by reality's tie

If I dare to spread my wings
I'm met with fleeting joyful things

Easily pulled back to the ground
Where harsh truths and sorrows abound

Should I choose to clip my own flight
I'll plummet from the swing's great height

Temporary joys, but pains endure
Grief grips my heart, so raw and pure

Tears cascade, a river of truth
While fleeting smiles offer respite,

Aloof I ransom myself to escape the mess
Seeking to change my prisoner's dress

Yet false comforts find their place
As fleeting pleasures briefly grace

Reality's weight is not embraced

By those who watch, their love misplaced

The force that once propelled my flight
Now weakened by their envious spite

They revel in my clipped wings' plight
As I yearn to take back my rightful height

But still, around me, wings unfurl
In harmony with my song and swirl

Carried by doves, my love takes flight
A testament to my enduring might

So I sit upon the swing, so still
Finding solace in the quiet's thrill

For though my flight may be clipped, it seems
I still can reach for my wildest dreams.

@Manu Adit
Dubai (UAE)

(POEM-32) Sunita Grover Raina & Babu Manukuladithyan.

SAIL THROUGH LIFE

Pick up your oar and let us go sailing
Would you like to row
Or leave it to the breeze
Let us once give it a chance
Ourselves we planned enough
Maybe things will be better hence
You worry it will drift us asunder
Our lives it will plunder
Just leave it in the hands of that wonder
He created us and doubt you him
Just surrender and trust
Things don't happen as per our whims
For many a boats with oars have drowned
And many with torn sails never been moaned
Enjoy life for nothing we own

@Sunita Grover Raina
India.

ECHOED BY HIM

Pick up your oar and let us go sailing
Upon the vast and restless sea
Shall we guide our fate with sturdy rowing
Or surrender to the wind's decree

Let's cast away our fears and doubts,
Embark on this uncertain quest

Embracing the unknown, we'll find our route
And let our hearts be truly blessed
For in the hands of the great wonder

We find our solace, hope, and trust
Surrendering to forces pulling us under
In the grand design, we are but dust

Let's not lament the lost or the owned,
But savor each moment, each fleeting tone
For life's treasures are not carved in stone
And in letting go, we may find our own

So let us sail with spirits high
Amidst the storms and gentle breeze
For in the journey, we may come to find
The beauty of life's mysteries.

@Manu Adit
Dubai (UAE)

(POEM-33) Sunita Grover Raina & Manu Adithyan.

IN PEACE I GO

You come jogging the same lane
Stop by the rose bush
But I am still a bud
You look at me fondle me lovingly
Inhale me
My fragrance cannot reach your heart yet dear
Your touch will bloom me early
I am waiting to open up to you
Keep patience
See today I shyly smile at you
And you are happy that my fragrance reached
your heart
Come tomorrow again dear
You will see my prettiest form
Do rub your cheeks with mine
And drop a few kisses before you go
I will be there for a day or more
You are getting married tomorrow
Let me attend your marriage
Fix me in the button hole of your tuxedo pocket
Let me rest on your chest

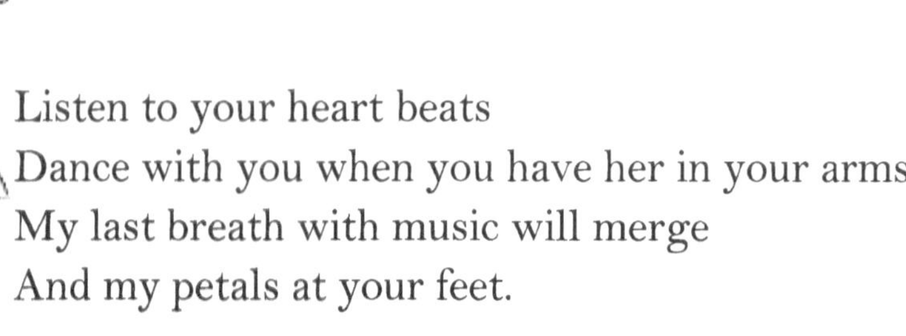

Listen to your heart beats
Dance with you when you have her in your arms
My last breath with music will merge
And my petals at your feet.

©Sunita Grover Raina
India.

ECHOED BY HIM

In the garden of love, a bud awaits
As the world whirls, in peaceful states

You come jogging, down the lane so fair
Pause by the rose bush, with tender care

A bud am I, in the morning dew
Yearning for the touch, that will make me new

You gaze upon me, with tender delight
Inhaling deeply, my fragrance so bright

But my essence, cannot reach your heart
For I am yet closed, waiting to depart

Your touch, dear friend, will awaken me
To bloom in beauty, for all to see

Patience, my love, for today I shyly smile
Tomorrow, my splendour will be in style

Embrace me then, with kisses so sweet
Before you wed, and your heart's complete

As you take her hand, and begin anew
Let me attend, to witness love so true

Fix me in your pocket, with tender care
Resting on your chest, I'll be close there

Listen to your heartbeats, as they play
Dance with you, in the light of day

My last breath, with music will merge
My petals, at your feet, a final surge.

@Manu Adit
Dubai (UAE)

NEED HIS REPLY

Hey sun ! did your scorching rays
Burn my jasmine essence on its way
He did not reply and I am in dismay

As to what could have happened,
I pray! Hey breeze !
Did you steal them for self
Or you gave my love to your friend elf
I am distraught not within myself
My soul is looking at the empty decanter on
shelf

But it has to reach just the right one
Not to be wasted on the wrong person

My perfume does not have a new version
That may be replaced to avoid my tension

I have reached the fag end of life in wait
Some more things to reach to him straight

Only you both know his home my dear mates
Only he can decode my letters and relate

Why is his reply not reaching me here
Hey breeze ! please help his reply to appear

My heart is panicking, nothing seems clear
My eyes are brimming, his welfare I fear

Reach it to me, even if his last letter
Let it be any news, I accept, still better

Our souls are free and not in fetters
If not this birth, then next will be our life setter.

©Sunita Grover Raina
India

ECHOED BY HIM

Under the sun's relentless gaze
she pleads
For her jasmine essence
lost in the breeze

But no reply comes
her heart in knots
Desperate for news
from the one she sought

Did the breeze carry her love away
Or did it gift her essence to the elf at play
Her soul in turmoil
lost and forlorn

Yearning for the love
that was once adorned
Her perfume
a timeless, unchanging token
Not to be replaced, not to be broken

She waits at life's fag end
with hope in sight
To reach the one
who holds her heart so tight

Breeze, carry his reply
on gentle wings

Ease her panicked heart
let hope take wings

Her eyes brim with worry
her soul in fear
Bring her the news,
let her heart adhere

Even if his last letter
fraught with sorrow
Any news will do,
she'll accept, tomorrow

Their souls are free
not bound by chains
In this life or next
destiny remains

So let the wind carry
her plea to his door
Let his reply bring solace
now and evermore.

@Manu Adit
Dubai (UAE)

MY CANVAS IS STILL BLANK

I suppose you dwell in everything.
Or are you everything?
I tried hard to visualize your form.
But I could not fit you in a form.
Lord Ravana's description of you, is all that is
known to me.
You do not have a beginning or an end.
A circle are you then?
I sit and think how should you look.
And the thinking goes on.
Are you those sounds which make no sense to
me.
Or those mystical sights that I get to see.
Or the fire within which none could tame
Or those tears that swell in ecstasy and pain.
Are you that void which fills my emptiness?
Or are you that nothing on which dwells the
existence of everything.
I tried to mingle with music, for if only I could
hear your Damru.
I tried dancing, for if only I could glimpse your
frequency.

I tried painting, for if only my brush would
move magically and bless me your sight.
My mind though in you has sank.
My canvas is still blank Oh! Shiva.

©Sunita Grover Raina
India

ECHOED BY HIM

Swirling thoughts and dreams
Where the boundaries of form

and essence seem to blur
I find myself lost in the search for you

In the dance of creation
in the whispers of the unseen

You elude my grasp
slip through my fingers like mist
A shape-shifter of divine mystery

I yearn to capture you
in the strokes of my imagination

But you, oh elusive muse
remain beyond my reach.
Do you dwell in the whispers of the wind
Or in the pulsing rhythms
of the earth's ancient heart

Perhaps you are the silence
between each beat
The space where all things find their birth
I seek you in the depths
of music's soulful embrace

In the tender caress
of a painter's brush

In the wild abandon of a dancer's leap
Yet still, my canvas remains blank
devoid of your essence
Oh, enigmatic Shiva

 You are the fire that burns within
The tears that flow in joy and sorrow
The void that fills my deepest emptiness
And the very foundation upon which existence
rests

So I continue to seek, to ponder, and to yearn
For in this journey, my spirit finds its wings
In the quest to capture your divine essence

My canvas may remain blank
but my soul is painted with your mystery.

@Manu Adit
Dubai (UAE)

(POEM-36) Sunita Grover Raina & Manu Adithyan.

DEAR BE FRANK

Let us dear be completely frank
How do we both exactly rank

In each other's curious eyes
Please do not my sweetheart lie

We are friends since many years
There should be no shyness or fears

Be bold daring and speak out
All your pent up locked thoughts

I am actually acting blind
I can dear clearly read your mind

Why do you doubt and hesitate
I no longer can patiently wait

You see me now as a lover
And so you do not want to hover

The change is very much obvious
You are no longer wild and devious

You even lost your sense of humour
Suddenly you are scared of rumours

You now dreamingly steal glances at me
When locked eyes game played we

Is this exciting change bothering you
I had switched my form long ago too

I did not know what to do
what to say
Lest you got scared and ran away

I am so happy to see your new form
Dear no longer can I be a lovelorn.

@Sunita Grover Raina
India

ECHOED BY HIM

In the dance of friendship's gentle sway
We've walked together, day by day

But now, my dear, the tides have turned
And love's sweet flame within us burned

Your eyes, once filled with laughter bright
Now hold a soft and tender light

No longer wild, no longer sly
Your heart now speaks, no need to pry

I've felt the change, I've seen the signs
The subtle shift, the tender lines

Of love that blooms, unspoken, true
Yet hesitates to break the view

You steal a glance, I catch your eye
In silent moments, love draws nigh

But still, a fear, a doubt, a woe
Lingers in the space we know

My dear, be frank, lay bare your heart
Let words and feelings freely start

For I, too, long to speak the truth
To bridge the gap, dispel the youth

In friendship's guise, love found its way
And now we stand at love's bouquet

So let us dare, no more delay
To let our hearts embrace love's sway

@Manu Adit
Dubai (UAE)

(POEM-37) Sunita Grover Raina & Manu Adithyan.

A Sad Affair

Be dedicated but not so engrossed
that life slowly passes you by
Glancing at you, hinting at you
to at least look at it.
If not love it.

And you unaware, were
counting your chickens
which never hatched
And what you achieved
was not what you wanted.

Life does not wait for you
to fulfil your wishes in future
For it has its own plans for you
But mind you it always reminds
And you did not pay heed to it
You kept putting things away

Now your planned time has come
to fulfil your wishes.

Life is standing and observing you
but your dreams look lifeless
and meaningless now.

For life has changed the sets.
For a body of 61 and a soul of 27.

The soul patiently remained waiting
and the body moved with time.

Go ahead, do what you wished,
says life.

The impatient young soul, now
wanting to tear apart your body.
Asking for freedom.
Asking you to fulfil its dreams.
Calling you a cheat.
As you could not keep your promise.

A sad affair.

©Sunita Grover Raina
India

ECHOED BY HIM

Life, so bittersweet,
We often lose sight
of the dreams we greet

Dedication leads
but don't be misled
Lest your heart's desires
be left unspread

The years slip by
with whispers so faint
Begging you to embrace life
and acquaint

Yourself with joys
that long to be found
Yet you, in your plans
were firmly bound

Now time stands still,
as your dreams await
But the stage has changed
it's not too late

Your youthful spirit
longing to be free
Calls out to you, to let it be

A body aged, a soul still young
The melody of life, left unsung

Open your heart
let your spirit rise
Fulfill your dreams, before time flies

The soul within, aching to soar
Yearning for the dreams it held before

Do not betray, do not deceive
But honor the promises you deeply believe

So heed the call, before it's too late
Let your spirit dance, embrace your fate

For life is patient, yet time does not wait
Embrace your dreams, before it's too late.

@Manu Adit
Dubai (UAE)

(POEM-38) Sunita Grover Raina & Manu Adithyan.

AGE IS NOT A BAR

Is love really dead
When age gradually spreads

Turning our hair grey
Many a wrinkle's wave

Seen here and there
What is there to fear

Says the sagging skin
It is not a sin

To grow with age old
Just be a bit bold

Move ahead in life
With no defeated sighs

Break your looking mirror
Think it to be
an eyesight error

For your inner self
Is still a young elf

With nothing dead within
Still wanting to swim

Towards the same desire
Love with the same fire

Go ahead and play
Keep making your hay

Till the sun shines
Keep craving for wines

It is just a thought in head
Love can never be dead

Age is not the culprit
It is the mind that
makes you unfit.

©Sunita Grover Raina
India

ECHOED BY HIM

Aging gracefully
with wisdom's grace

Love knows no bounds
nor does it tire
It burns eternal
a never-ending fire

As years pass by
and youth takes flight
Our spirits soar
still shining bright

With each laugh line
and silver strand
We embrace the beauty
of where we stand

Love's flame flickers
but never dies
It lights the path
beneath aging skies

For in our hearts
the passion lives
On a timeless force
from dusk till dawn

So let the mirror crack
and splinter
For true beauty
lies in love's sweet center

Age is but a number
a fleeting guise
Love knows no limits
it never dies.

@Manu Adit
Dubai (UAE)

(POEM-39) Sunita Grover Raina & Manu Adithyan.

ARDHANAREESHVARA

Just came out from within
The true picture of being
Loving oneself means
Loving the other half
In all resides
Ardhanareeshvara
Lord Shiva ishvara
Purusha Prakriti
Allowed Parvati
To reside within him
Embracing limb to limb
So are we his parts
Within us the two halves
Every man has his woman within
And in every woman her him
Loving oneself means
Loving the other half

©Sunita Grover Raina
India

ECHOED BY HIM

In the dance of cosmic embrace,
Ardhanareeshvara, in boundless grace

A union of halves, a divine melding
Where man and woman find their dwelling

In every beating heart, a hidden twin
Bound in spirit, entwined within

Purusha and Prakriti, as one they dwell
In the depths of our being, a timeless spell

Loving oneself, a quest to behold
A mirror of unity, a story untold

For in the depths of our soul's design
Man and woman entwine, a love so fine

Embracing limb to limb, in silent repose
Ardhanareeshvara, where harmony flows

In every soul, the two halves entwine
A symphony of love, an eternal sign

So let us seek within, with eyes to see
The Ardhanareeshvara, the unity

For loving oneself means, in truth to find
The other half within, the union divine.

@Manu Adit
Dubai (UAE)

(POEM-40) Sunita Grover Raina & Manu Adithyan.

AT TIMES

At times I do nothing
And in this nothingness
I kept finding lost things

At times I can't sleep
And in this awakeness
I see lovely dreams

At times I sit in silence
And as silence talks
I create love poems

At times I appear mad
As madness surrounds me
I see the road to heaven

At times I wish to know all
My thoughts did call
All boomeranged within.

©Sunita Grover Raina
India

ECHOED BY HIM

In depths of stillness
lost things are found
Amidst the quiet
dreams in wakefulness abound

Silence speaks in whispers
love poems take flight
Madness unveils the road
to heavens bright

In longing to grasp all
thoughts echo and roam
Yet answers evade
and circles lead back home

For in life's tangled web
wisdom may elude
And our quest for understanding
 remains unsubdued.

@Manu Adit
Dubai (UAE)

(POEM-41) Sunita Grover Raina & Manu Adithyan.

ATTACHMENTS LEAD TO PAIN

Attachments of all types
lead to pain
Very easily they do slain

Get blackmailed,
Your emotions
Leaving you in doldrums

You sit and wonder
where you went wrong
Wrong you were not
but thought you did belong

All relations are virtual
Do not get deceived
that blood rules

For souls if connect
They never suspect

They never inspect
They never disrespect

142

I connect readily
Try to move steadily

A fool in this world
Only to be twirled

Around for some time
For every relation
stops to chime

Somewhere and
at sometime
Your realization,
to it resigns

You felt proud
to hold all together
Your cap is loaded
with such false feathers

Keep deceiving your
already deceived within
Hope and expectations are
balancing on threads thin

They will get you
no where dear
For destiny reins
are held elsewhere

Safer to get attached to
surrounding nature
The same face of seasons
is shown every year

Attachments to things at times
become a burden
If no one to care for them
looks certain

Desperately you try
to give them away
To needy and those who
will care and not sway

Accept the truth and
try to move away
Do not to such attachments
get attached and stay

For attachments of all types
lead to pain
Very easily they do slain

©Sunita Grover Raina
India

145

ECHOED BY HIM

Attachments, soft whispers of the heart
Entwined with joy, but never truly apart

Yet chains of longing, lead to pain
In a world where emotions wane

Blackmailed by feelings, held in sway
Lost in the depths of emotional dismay

We sit and ponder where we went wrong
Yet the fault lies not where we belong

Relations, both real and virtual, deceive
As blood's bond fails to relieve

But when souls connect, they suspect naught
Nor do they inspect, nor ever resort to fraught

I connect readily, hoping to transcend
Unaware, I'm but a fool, destined to bend

For every relation, time will cease its chime
And in that moment, realization will climb

Proudly we hold on, with false feathers adorned,
Deceiving ourselves, in a world forlorn.

Hope and expectations, precariously balanced
Destined to lead us on, our fate unchallenged

Safer, perhaps, to embrace nature's embrace
Where seasons reveal their unchanging face

Attachments to things, a burden they may
become
When care is absent and hearts grow numb

Desperate to give, to those who will cherish
To unburden the soul, and no longer perish.

@Manu Adit
Dubai (UAE)

(POEM-42) Sunita Grover Raina & Manu Adithyan.

BREEZE I WANT TO BE

I have now covered
thousands of miles
Stuck to my face are some
true and fake smiles

Let positive vibes
from me always flow
Though negative vibes at me
they love to throw

You filled me with a strange love
to which I had to agree
But then why did you give me
those eyes that strangely see

With one less maybe my life
 would have been better
I too might have been
a fast go getter

I am calling since ages,
now confused at what
At times I hear a voice saying
you already have got

But I am still searching
for that one needed glance
Which would hypnotize me
in an eternal trance

My eyes that do see
will then, turn blind
On the roads I walk, will have
nothing left to find

Turn me mad, turn me into
that sweet smelling breeze
Let there be no barriers,
let time too with me freeze

Without these eyes
I will truly be free
My fragrance jasmine
will mingle with fragrance thee

Tired I am now
of my thoughts distraught
Free me from all of these
oughts and naughts.

©Sunita Grover Raina
India

ECHOED BY HIM

Gentle seeker of the breeze
Your words paint a restless tale
Of miles travelled and smiles worn
Of love strange and eyes that unveil

You long for release, for freedom true
From the burdens of sight and sound
To drift as a sweet, fragrant zephyr
Unbound by earthly bounds

Your yearning echoes in the wind
As it whispers through the trees
Seeking solace in a timeless dance
Yearning for a soul's release

Let the breeze take you in its embrace
And carry you to tranquil heights
Where worries fade and burdens lift
And the soul takes peaceful flights

Embrace the freedom that awaits
In the sweet, scented air
Let the whispers of the world surround
And free you from all care

Soar as the breeze you long to be
Invisible, yet ever near
Embracing the world with gentle touch
And easing every fear.

@Manu Adit. Dubai (UAE)

(POEM-43) Sunita Grover Raina & Manu Adithyan.

BROKEN WINGS

They come to me
for care and die
Be it birds
or butterflies

Something they come
to leave behind
For these thoughts do come
to me, remind

Happening this is
since many years
When they leave
I shed some salty tears

But this is true,
this my willing choice
Let others
in their ways rejoice

I want to see them
dance and sing

Try best to mend
these broken wings

In heart I know
cannot much help
Still try my best,
they think me elf

They come to me
for care and die
Be it birds
or butterflies.

©Sunita Grover Raina
India

ECHOED BY HIM

In the garden of broken wings,
Where sorrow and hope take flight
A tender soul tends to the fallen things
Embracing darkness with a guiding light

Birdsong fades into the twilight air
But the caretaker's heart, it stays alight
For in the midst of the deepest despair
Hope blooms, fragile but bright

Whispers of wind carry tales untold
Of creatures that sought solace in the tender
hand
In the caretaker's heart, a story unfolds
Of love and loss upon this fleeting land

A dance of life and death, a bittersweet
symphony
Eternal cycle of joy and pain
Yet in the midst of this poignant elegy
The caretaker finds purpose to remain

Broken wings and fragile dreams
In the shelter of gentle hands they lay

A testament to love's enduring seams
In the caretaker's heart, they'll always stay.

@Manu Adit
Dubai (UAE)

(POEM-44) Sunita Grover Raina & Manu Adithyan.

DANCE IN DARKNESS

Could the stars remove
the darkness of night

Could the fireflies
make a dark night bright

They Just a flickering glitter
to behold

To distract you from the light
the darkness holds

Ever was I scared
of darkness

The mind a culprit
to its starkness

Diverted thoughts
to the small shines

When in the darkness were hidden
diamond mines

It is only when you lose
all your fears

You get to see things in life
crystal clear

life went on lashing
marked and bruised me

Till in desperation
I made it my enemy

Challenged it openly
and jumped into burning pits

And found life with arms open,
smiling at my humour less wit

It was slowly luring me
to react and to act

And in these reactions
see all the true facts

In a painful way
it murdered all my fears

In the darkness made me
shed a lot of tears

Saw to it that
no one would wipe them

Let them slide and made me
lick the salted gems

Count yourself blessed
to be tutored by life

What I was scared of
actually removed my strife

My true friends were the ones
who scared me

Oh! life, darkness I welcome
and in it, now all clearly see.

©Sunita Grover Raina
India

ECHOED BY HIM

Amidst the starry tapestry,
Could the darkness ever flee

Could the fireflies' gentle light
Chase away the solemn night

Yet in the flickering glow, we find
A fleeting refuge for the mind

A respite from the shadows deep
Where hidden treasures lie asleep

Once I trembled in its grasp
The darkness, with its chilling clasp

My thoughts, conspiring with the night
Magnified each fearful plight

But when I dared to face the dark
To wander through its daunting arc

Life's lessons began to unfold
In the mysteries it gently told

Battered by life's relentless storm
I made darkness my sworn form

Challenging it with fearless might
Plunging into its depths, taking flight

As it beckoned me to engage
I learned to read life's cryptic page

In its painful embrace, I found release
And shed my fears, finding inner peace

Tears flowed freely in its embrace
Unwiped, they left a salty trace

Life's tutor, in darkness' shroud,
Unveiled truths, both harsh and proud

Those who once scared me, I now see
As friends who set my spirit free

Oh life, oh darkness, I welcome your call
For within you, I've found my all.

@Manu Adit
Dubai (UAE)

(POEM-45) Sunita Grover Raina & Manu Adithyan.

DEAR GOD

For what did you create us Dear God
And you are going on doing so non stop

This earth has become a dump ground of humans
Very soon we won't be able to lie down
We will suffocate to death

Are you planning to shuttle us to Moon
If so then please take me in the first lot

I always wished I was living there and not here
Surely you must have kept count of our wishes
And I will pass your test

By the way which planet are you residing on
Would I be able to view that from Moon

Must be very beautiful as you stay there
And I have started wishing to stay there too

Dear God do you give double promotions
Then I will work hard on it

Leave the Moon I now target your home
Your home would be a heaven

And if you gave triple promotions
Let me know soon

For then I will aim straight for your heart
And forget all about Moon.

©Sunita Grover Raina
India

ECHOED BY HIM

Dear soul in search of purpose and meaning,
Let your heart be open to the cosmic gleaming
For in this vast expanse of time and space
We are but stardust, bound to this earthly place

Dear seeker, within you lies a universe untold
A symphony of dreams waiting to unfold
Though this world may seem a burden to bear
Look beyond, find the magic that's rare

Let the moonlight guide your weary soul
As you envision a destination, your ultimate goal
But dear one, remember, in your quest divine
The home of God resides in every heartbeat, every sign

So seek not the moon, nor distant starry skies
For within you, the divine essence lies
Embrace the journey, embrace the unknown
For in love and kindness, you shall find your own.

@Manu Adit
Dubai (UAE)

(POEM-46) Sunita Grover Raina & Manu Adithyan.

DREAMS ALWAYS DIES

Hey dream!
Why do you run away?
Why do you wake me
and leave me thirsty

Yes you run away so fast
That by the time I am awake
Nothing lasts

Just a bit of taste
you leave behind
Either sad or happy
I myself find

Hey dream
stay for some time
Let me see
your complete form
Why are you so moody?

Sad I feel
when it was a romantic reel
I moving with my hero
And you erase my memory to zero

Are you
a psychopath killer
Who turns things
into a thriller
And then suddenly lights the screen
And pop! Goes my dream

With years I did try
to hold on to you
Half awake and half sleepy mode
is how I grew
Still you escaped my grip
Easily from my hands slipped

I really do not know
how to you
mend
Determined I am
to see you once
till the end

At times
I feel
that too will be my end

Never to rudely awake
Never will I quake or shake
See a dream with no break

Will be a peaceful deadly sleep
In dreams engrossed deep
Either a hell or heaven
it will be.

©Sunita Grover Raina
India

ECHOED BY HIM

In the dreams, I wander lost
Chasing shadows that slip away

Like fleeting whispers in the frost
They leave me yearning, in disarray

Oh, elusive dreams, why do you flee
Why tantalize, then disappear

You dance before my eyes, wild and free
Then vanish, leaving me in fear

Your fleeting touch, a bittersweet tease
A fleeting taste of joy or sorrow

Like a cruel jest, you come and please
Then fade, leaving a void to borrow

Are you a trickster, a fickle sprite
Playing games with my weary mind

Or a gentle muse, veiled in the night

Whose elusive nature I cannot bind

 I long to hold you, to see you clear
To grasp the essence of your flight

But you slip through my fingers, my dear
Leaving me yearning in the night

Yet still I strive to capture your grace
To hold you close, to understand

For in your depths, I seek a trace
Of truth and beauty, hand in hand

So let me dream, unbroken, unbound
In peaceful slumber, let me keep

In dreams, a solace that can be found
A refuge where my soul can sleep.

@Manu Adit
Dubai (UAE)

(POEM-47) Sunita Grover Raina & Manu Adithyan.

EROTICA!

Erotica!
yes write about erotica

You want to sexually
arouse a reader
You want to be
an erotica breeder

Go ahead with clean words
you do
Dear can you?

Without bringing in boobs and thighs
And false kisses and false sighs!

You can still
make them swoon
Into each others arms
to bloom

Get them entangled
like vines
Make their eyes
like diamonds shine

Give birth to dreams
of love making
Hearts for each other
craving and aching

Let your erotica
touch their souls
Then light their organs
as a goal

There is surely
lust in love
Let there also be
love in lust love

There are enough
of sickening porn clips
That murdered love
with easy, quick strips

A few minutes of
these disgusting sights
Gives birth to repulsion
despite

Let me see you
me ignite
Those cheap words of feelings
give a fright

For a glance of your lover
slight
Is enough to get the hormones
flow in delight.

And make you think will it be
tonight.

©Sunita Grover Raina
India

ECHOED BY HIM

Passion's artistry
Where words ignite the soul's mystery
I'll paint a picture, pure and true
Of love and longing, just for you

No need for crass or vulgar verse
No need for lines that only curse
The sacred bond that two hearts share
In tender moments, oh so rare

Let my verses weave a tale of love
A dance of spirits, hand in glove
Where yearning blooms like fragile flowers
In secret gardens, whispered hours

A symphony of tender touch
A gentle yearning, oh so much
To kindle flames that softly burn
And leave our souls forever yearn

So come with me, let's write a song
Of love that's deep and true and strong
And let our words, like gentle rain
Awaken hearts to love again.

@Manu Adit
Dubai (UAE)

(POEM-48) Sunita Grover Raina & Manu Adithyan.

EXTRA MARITAL AFFAIR

A matter to think about
With a cool mind
Why people get entangled in them
Surely not for fun

For there are ways which society
has made specially for men
Existing openly
Throughout world
And they do not soil
the pure nuptial knots

Only women spoil them

Society has not given
them such licensed places to go openly
It is taboo as only men are
flesh and blood
And women born saints
with no desires or emotions

But if two pure souls
tortured in love
Crave love and share feelings
and find solace in each other

172

to live this life with some peace
It is a big crime they do

Labelled extra marital affair

Yes an affair but still not a crime
Why does this pinch both the genders more
This extra marital affair

When rapes
Sexual torture of women
and brothels flourish

And they are quiet about it

Think with a cool mind
It is because of jealousy
For they crave it too
They too live in the debris
of their relations
They too want love
but do not have the guts
So it is labelled a no no
as they could not get it

As they could not step out

No crime they do these people
They just collect some love and go
back to their

crumbled relations due to other attachments
waiting at home

Fulfilling their duties
and keeping themselves alive
by these bits and pieces of love
they share within themselves.

An extra relation they dare to tread
Though labelled married
attaching another label to their souls.

They have a life to live too.
They have a right to live too.

Extra marital affair
A name unfair
For a relation in despair to repair
Lost love and flow of tears

©Sunita Grover Raina
India

ECHOED BY HIM

In the tangled web of human hearts
A dance of love, a game of parts
Where society's rules draw lines so stark
And passions flame against the dark

 A matter to ponder, cool and clear
Why this entanglement, this fear
For love knows not the bounds we bind
Yet society's gaze is unforgiving, unkind

Men, with their spaces, open and wide
Allowed to wander, to cast aside
While women are tethered, to vows and to home
Their desires and emotions condemned to roam

But what of two souls, pure and true
Bound by a love that society misconstrues
Their hearts entwined, seeking solace and peace
In a world where love's restrictions never cease

Labelled as crime, this affair of the heart
Yet why does it sting, tear genders apart
In a world where violence and vice run rife
This love is condemned, a silent strife

Think with a cool mind, let reason unfurl
It's jealousy masked, that makes society swirl
For they too yearn, they too ache and desire
But lack the courage to set their love on fire

No crime in collecting love's tender embrace
In a world where affection is a scarce and
precious grace
So let not the labels weigh heavy or snare
For love is love, in this extra marital affair

Let the soul of compassion be our guiding light
To understand, to embrace, to make wrongs
right
For in the depths of love, pure and rare
There lies the truth of this extra marital affair

@Manu Adit
Dubai (UAE)

(POEM-49) Sunita Grover Raina & Manu Adithyan.

Flowers Bloom On Ground

When my wings seemed clipped
I wanted to fly

I did flutter to shorter heights
Could have flown
To see brighter sights
But something said
For you not right

Wait and watch
Let not wings torch
With small pleasures
Which appear a treasure

I fluttered back
to my open cage
Many stories I typed
on my life's page

Now my wings have grown
New wings not shown

Many wines I sipped
Still never tripped

Green pastures call
My past, I recall

I can easily fly
And give it a try

But I sit tight
Observing the plight
How clipped wings fight.

Why did I not fly?

For I had wings of
Butterfly.

Flowers bloom on ground
and not in sky.

©Sunita Grover Raina
India.

ECHOED BY HIM

In the garden of life
I longed to soar high
But fate whispered softly
"Not yet, don't defy."

I yearned for the heavens
to touch the azure
Yet something unseen
held me back, unsure.

I danced in the breeze
but my flight was brief
Held back by a force
a lingering belief.

Should I have soared far
to realms unknown?
Or cherish the moments
within my own zone?

I returned to my haven
my heart's dwelling place
Penned tales of my journey
with elegance and grace.

My wings, once fragile
now stronger than before
Yearning for the skies
Craving to explore.

Amidst life's sweet nectar
I tread with care
Savouring each sip
without a stumble or snare.

The meadows beckon
recalling days gone by
Yet I remain grounded
pondering the why.

Why did I not soar
with the wind's gentle sigh?

With wings of a butterfly
meant to touch the sky.

Yet I find solace in blossoms
on earth they're found
For in their humble beauty
true grace is crowned.

So I sit and I watch
as clipped wings take flight

A silent observer
in the soft evening light.

Embracing the beauty
in all that's around
For flowers bloom on the ground
not in the sky's bound.

@Manu Adit
Dubai (UAE)

(POEM-50) Sunita Grover Raina & Manu Adithyan.

IN ANKLET I BEAT

Let me be the anklet
tied to your feet
I want to dance endlessly
at our every meet

While You create
the universe
Add verse after verse
to it
I will hold tightly on
to your feet

Every day will I get
to greet
your feet

I feel replete
at your feet

Do not untie
this bond

Or I die
at your feet

My need will
remain
incomplete

You dance and dance
While I in trance
Will hold on
to your feet

Lost in the music
you create
Lost in every beat
Adding my little bit
I fearfully entreat

Let me be the anklet
tied to your feet
Oh! Shiva.

©Sunita Grover Raina
India.

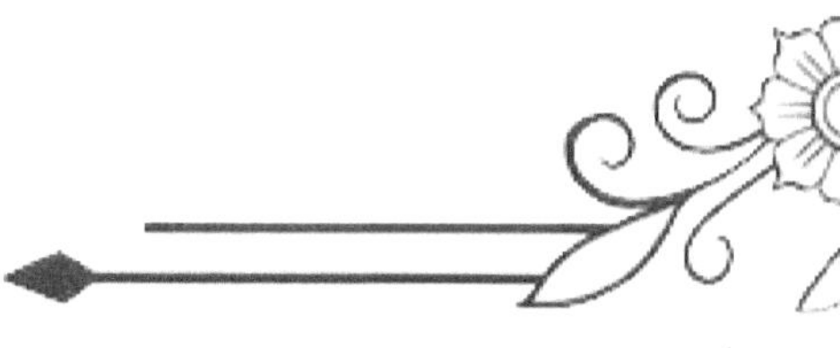

ECHOED BY HIM

In anklet's gentle chime
I find my place
Bound to your steps
in endless embrace

With each move
a universe is born
I cling, I dance
from eve to morn

Your feet, my solace
my sacred shrine
In their grace
my purpose, my design

Yet, fear grips me
a haunting decree
Unravel this bond
and I cease to be

In your rhythm
I find my plea
Lost in the melody
of eternity

Wrapped in your dance
a timeless feat
Let me be the anklet
at your feet

Oh, Shiva
in your cosmic trance
Grant me the chance
to dance, to dance

For in your steps
my essence, complete
Let me be the anklet
at your feet.

@Manu Adit
Dubai (UAE)

Author Bio

Sunita **G**rover **R**aina, born on the 21st of November in 1959, hails originally from the picturesque town of Srinagar, Jammu and Kashmir, India. She occupies the position of the third offspring to her esteemed Kashmiri Pandit parents. Her formative years were spent amidst the cultural richness of Kolkata, West Bengal, where she received her education.

Amidst the vibrant corridors of education, Sunita Grover Raina blossomed. She embarked on her academic journey at the prestigious Ashok Hall Girls Higher Secondary School, nurturing her intellect and character. Her scholastic journey culminated with distinction as she graduated with an honour's degree in B Pharmacy from Jadavpur University in Kolkata, a testament to her dedication and commitment.

Her professional journey commenced in 1983 when she joined the esteemed ranks of the government service in West Bangal. Over the years, she ascended the ladder of her career with unwavering determination and grace, ultimately retiring in 2019 as the Director of Drugs Control for the state of West Bengal.

Sunita's personal life is imbued with a deep and enduring connection to the late Anil Grover, a renowned journalist, whom she married in the year 1984. Their union was blessed with the gift of a son, Akshar Grover, who continues to be a source of joy and pride.

Music courses through her veins, infusing her life with its enchanting melodies. Yet, it is her journey as a poet that has truly captivated the world's attention. Since March 2021, Sunita has emerged as a prolific and multi-award-winning poet. Her poems have left an indelible mark on the literary landscape, dazzling readers and critics alike with their exquisite craftsmanship.

Sunita's poetic expression is characterized by a rare lyrical fluidity, a gift possessed by only a select few in the contemporary literary world. Her pen dances across a myriad of subjects, embracing the entire spectrum of human experience. Yet, her poetic heart gravitates towards the themes of passion, life, and love, painting them with hues that resonate with the depths of the human soul. Sunita Grover Raina, the poet, is a beacon of creativity and a testament to the power of artistry to touch hearts and inspire minds.

Manu Adit, **Manu Adithyan**, was born on the
15th of March 1969 in the charming town of Pala,
nestled within Kottayam District, Kerala. He is the
youngest among four siblings. His parents, both
dedicated government officers in the state of Kerala,
instilled in him a sense of purpose from an early age.

Adit's schooling was completed in Pala, his educational
journey later took him to colleges under Mahatma
Gandhi University in Kerala. There, he earned a degree
in Physics. His insatiable thirst for knowledge led him to
explore the fields of business and financial management,
where he attained professional certifications from the
Institute of Cost Accountants of India and the Institute
of Management Accountants of the USA, in addition to
securing a Post Graduate Diploma in Business
Administration.

In 1994, he embarked on his professional career at Oli
Palm India Ltd, marking the beginning of his corporate
journey. Subsequently, he joined the esteemed ranks of
the oldest Malayalam newspaper, Deepika Daily, and
steadily ascended the ranks, eventually assuming the role
of Finance Manager for the group of publications in
2002. His insatiable ambition prompted him to explore
international opportunities, leading to his departure from
Rashtra Deepika Ltd in 2004. He found a new
professional home at Jacobsons, Dubai, where he
currently serves as the Head of Finance Administration
and HR functions.

Adit's personal life is intertwined with his soulmate, Soya Adithya, a highly educated individual with postgraduate qualifications in Economics and a Bachelor of Education. Their partnership adds depth and vibrancy to his life.

From childhood, Adit harboured a profound admiration for the world of poetry. Although blessed with innate writing skills, he did not initially pursue poetry as a profession or passion. It was only when he became part of poetic groups in the online realm that he began responding to the verses that crossed his path, infusing them with his poetic essence. Encouragement from fellow poets ignited his confidence, prompting him to engage actively in forums, where he swiftly garnered poetry awards.

Adit's poetic creations are marked by their spontaneity and masterful craftsmanship. He possesses the rare ability to explore a myriad of topics, yet his heart remains inclined towards addressing the burning human problems of our time. In the realm of poetry, he is a force to be reckoned with, lending his voice to the pressing issues that define our existence.

www.ingramcontent.com/pod-product-compliance
Lightning Source LLC
Chambersburg PA
CBHW031130130726
47988CB00006B/2300